By a woman who finds excitement in your life and
business, fueled by an abundance of passion and
prosperity.

Change a Smile
Change a Life

Stephanie Welker

MY STORY

I had a bit of a rough childhood. No father around until I was a young adult. An alcoholic mother with abusive boyfriends and drinking binges leaving my brother and I to fend for ourselves for days at a time. Poor dental care was an understatement. At 15, I began living on my own.

In my early 20s, browsing the classifieds, I found two main job offerings: accounting and dental positions. Dental work required the least amount of schooling, time, and money to land a decent-paying job and, a major perk, potentially free dental care. Little did I know, this was the start of a completely new life.

YOUR STORY

Out of all the paths you could have chosen in life, you decided to become a dental business owner. In my opinion, that was an incredible choice. It is a powerful opportunity to change lives while building a prosperous future for yourself. Here is the catch: you develop the skill set, but do you have the business mindset?

THE PEPTALK

You've invested time, money, and dedication to complete dental school. You have the skills to transform smiles, and, by extension, change lives. Now, you need the business knowledge and guidance to run your practice in a way that creates wealth, success, and balance in your life.

The million-dollar practice is within reach, if you are disciplined and dedicated to YOURSELF and YOUR BUSINESS.

Think about it: what is the point of becoming a dentist and owning your own practice if you are going to work your entire life with nothing to show for it? You could just be like the average American, but you are not, you are a business owner. You have the opportunity to build an extraordinary life. Even if you are experienced, there is still time to make changes and commit to creating a better future for yourself.

I believe you would not be reading this book if your business, personal bank account, and life were exactly as you envisioned them. Utilize this book as your guide. Flip through the chapters, set goals, take notes, and return to the book often. Do not give up on yourself or your business.

"Success truly begins the day you wake up deciding to be Successful"

- *Stephanie Welker*

Table of Contents

SECTION ONE:

SET YOURSELF UP FOR SUCCESS

SECTION 1

Life After Dental

In dentistry, it is often mentioned that treatment planning with patients leads to higher acceptance rates. The reason? People tend to make decisions based on emotions. When we design the outcome from the start, showing patients the potential of their perfect smile, it creates feelings of joy and excitement. Those positive emotions, more often than not, lead patients to say, *"YES."*

Well, now it is your turn to say, *"Yes"* to your own treatment plan, for your life and your business. Life After Dental is all about designing your retirement at the start of this new chapter. Whether you are just beginning or a seasoned business owner, it is never too late to start fresh. Each of us have the power to wake up tomorrow and choose to do better, be better, and have more.

The goal from this day forward is to set yourself up for success based on how you want to live your life. If you could close your eyes right now and daydream about living

with total freedom, financial and otherwise, what would that look like to you? Would you travel the world?
Would you buy your dream home, debt-free?

In later chapters we will discuss your full Retirement Plan. We will cover how you plan to retire, what steps are necessary, at what age you would like to retire, and more. They are the "How" chapters. This is the "*Why*" chapter, the incentive and motivation behind it all.

When we are young, we dream of becoming someone big, like a movie star or a doctor, and of having big things, like expensive cars or a grand house. The thought of being whoever we wanted to be and having whatever we wanted to have is thrilling.

Just for a moment, allow yourself to dream.

Take a moment to jot down what total freedom would look like for you.

_____

_____

_____

_____

_____

_____

_____

_____

_____

_____

_____

_____

_____

_____

It can be the present or future, list some things you would like to accomplish in your life.

_____

_____

_____

_____

_____

_____

_____

_____

_____

_____

_____

_____

_____

Lastly, create a list of a few things you would like to do AFTER retirement.

_____

_____

_____

_____

_____

_____

_____

_____

_____

_____

As you go through this book, carry the feelings from your dreams with you. Be intentional.

Personal Goals

When you decided to attend dental school and complete your studies, what was your reasoning? What was it that brought you joy when thinking of working on a person's smile?

Sit down in a quiet space with a spiral notebook. This will be your reflection journal. **Write down:**

- *How you envision your ideal practice, business, or company running*
- *The layout of your operatories*
- *Your approach to hygiene, do you have multiple hygienist?*
- *Do you have associates or work solo?*
- *What technology you want to incorporate*
- *Additional skills you would like to acquire or develop*

❖ *Consider the following:*
- *What procedure excites you the most?*
- *What kind of culture do you want to create in your office?*
- *How profitable will your ideal business be?*
- *How much will you pay yourself?*

The most successful dental business owners see the endgame from the beginning. Look at this as a treatment plan for both your business and your personal future.

You must stay engaged. Set goals. Schedule appointments with yourself. Hold meetings with your team. Challenge yourself. Challenge your team. Always maintain the mindset: This is MY business, MY money, MY family's money, and MY retirement. There is no backup. The only person you can rely on 100%, is you. And the reality is, you could live 20 years after retirement. At 93, my Nan is still mentally sound, good health, no walker, driving her car, and is living on her own in her family home. God willing, you could very well live into your 90's.

While that resonates, here is another nugget, the more you invest in yourself and your team, the better the culture you will create. When you foster a valued culture, you build a team that wants to work with you, and for you. The more you have to offer, health benefits, profit sharing, and 401(k) plans, the better-quality people you will attract.

As we move forward, we will set goals, break down those goals into manageable steps for the coming year, conduct self and team evaluations, brainstorm new money-making ideas, and discover what truly makes you happy in dentistry. I am excited to take this journey with you, especially the chapter on Wealth in Beauty, which, in my opinion, every dental office should consider incorporating a beauty line. It elevates the practice.

Isn't it wonderful that you have the power to make your practice and business exactly what you desire?

Are you ready to invest in you and create a fortune, while maintaining a balanced personal life?

Putting in the work, being intentional with every decision you make, and showing up for yourself will create the multimillion-dollar business you dream about.

Do not waste this incredible opportunity you have been given.

Personal Goals/To do list

_____

_____

_____

_____

_____

_____

_____

_____

_____

_____

_____

_____

_____

_____

_____

_____

_____

_____

_____

_____

_____

_____

_____

Team

This is the tough love chapter. Implementing these suggestions will be challenging, but it will be worth it. Following through will create the culture every practice needs to have. Do not give up. I encourage you to embrace this process and remember:

"If you want to be rich, sometimes you have to be a bitch."

No matter where you are in your career, start by setting aside specific times and days to interview your team. You are going to offer them a lot, so you should expect a lot in return. You want a team that is genuinely motivated to work for you.

They must care deeply about their role, your patients, and the success of the practice. Their priorities should include treatment plan fulfillment, recalls, social media, collections, insurance satisfaction and, most importantly, their own professional growth. Team members must show up on time, ready to give their best every day. They should have the drive to go the extra mile, maintain a positive attitude, and contribute as true team players.

Do not settle. Do not be afraid to let people go if they do not meet your expectations. At the same time, do not shy away from paying top performers slightly more than their market value. That extra investment will pay off in the long run through increased revenue, happier staff, and more satisfied, loyal patients.

This approach will also lead to less turnover, better treatment plan fulfillment, and a smoother-running business overall. Adopt a win-win mindset: if you invest in your team, they will invest in you.

Caveat: You must create structure and lead with example while being stern when necessary. This is why it is crucial to take the time to define how big you want your office to grow and how you envision your business running.

❖ **Set your goals:**
- How many hygiene rooms will you need?
- What is the ideal size of your front office staff?
- Do you want one person handling social media, reviews, and recalls?
- How many operatories do you plan to run, and how many assistants will it take to support your schedule effectively?

- If you have or plan to have associates, will they need dedicated teams to manage their schedules?

To ensure a smooth workflow, each doctor should have their own back-office assistant or team, supplemented by a cross-trained floater to handle call-outs and vacations. The same principle applies to the front office staff. This structure keeps the workflow consistent and minimizes confusion.

If possible, assign each assistant to a specific operatory. This gives them control over their space and prevents unnecessary headaches.

Suggestions and considerations

- What are the dental state laws? What tasks can assistants and hygienists perform independently?
- What certifications are they eligible to obtain? Are you willing to cover certification costs with contingencies?
- What benefits can you offer your team? Consider options such as health insurance, retirement plans, quarterly or holiday

bonuses, advancement opportunities, cross-training, or access to new technology.

When onboarding new team members, have a structured training program in place. To maximize efficiency, ensure your team is well-trained in:

- Technology
- Implants
- Sterilization protocols
- CPR/AED
- Radiology
- Clear aligners
- Treatment plan acceptance
- Health histories
- Your Patient Management Software

Allow your team to feel important. The more knowledgeable your team is, the smoother your business will run, and the more valued your team will feel. Have you heard the saying, *"Knowledge is power"*? It applies to your team as well. Knowledgeable people feel important. People who feel important become confident. Confident individuals tend to be more positive. More positive people contribute to a more uplifting office culture. Do you see how it all connects?

That said, maintain boundaries. Be firm, but approach situations kindly. Clearly define each team member's role and set clear expectations. Remember, you are not their friend, you are running a business. Change can be difficult for some people. Ask yourself: are they willing to work with you or are they working against you?

You can demonstrate your appreciation for your team while still running a tight ship. Ultimately, it is your responsibility to keep your team trained, accountable, and aligned with your goals.

"A leader isn't someone who forces others to make him stronger; a leader is someone willing to give his strength to others so that they may have the strength to stand on their own."

-Beth Revis

Team Goals/To do list

_____

_____

_____

_____

_____

_____

_____

_____

_____

_____

_____

_____

_____

_____

_____

_____

_____

_____

_____

_____

_____

_____

Game Plan

Let's create the practice of your dreams, the one that brings you both financial success and work-life balance. Start by writing down your goals and placing them somewhere you can see every day.

❖ **Here are some goals to consider:**

- What percentage of your profits will you set aside each pay period to invest in yourself and your business?
- What new skills do you need to learn?
- What technology could enhance your day-to-day operations?
- Is it time to revamp your website?

As you work through this book, let yourself brainstorm freely. Capture your ideas as they come, use a notes app on your phone or keep a journal nearby.

❖ **Try this exercise:**

Think back to the moment you decided to become a dentist.

- How did you feel in that moment?
- What excited you the most?
- How did you imagine your future practice?

- Which dental school skill did you enjoy the most?
- Which skill made you uncomfortable, and how can you improve on it?

Tap into those memories and emotions as you move forward with your new game plan. No matter where you are in your career, you can choose today to make changes for a better future.

Take a few days, or even a few weeks, to reflect on this section. Set realistic, actionable goals. Do not shy away from dreaming big. The bigger, the better.

Say to yourself: **From this moment on...**

- I am going to set aside 10% of my earnings into a High-Yield Money Market account.
- *I am going to increase gross profit by implementing XYZ.*
- *I am going to let go of staff who do not align with my vision and reward those who go the extra mile.*
- *I am going to be unapologetically selfish when it comes to running my business the way I see fit.*

- *I am going to thank my staff every day.*
- *I am going to thank each patient for choosing to trust me with their care.*
- *I am going to hold myself accountable for turning both my business and personal goals into reality.*
- *I am going to be the best business owner, boss, doctor, and patient care provider I can be.*

From this day forward:

- *I will run my business with the end game in mind.*
- *I will make running my business my top priority.*
- *I promise myself I will not work my entire life with nothing to show for it.*

"Armatures sit and wait for inspiration, the rest of us just get up and go to work."

-Stephen King

Game Plan: To do List

Retirement Goals:

_____

_____

_____

_____

_____

_____

_____

_____

_____

Personal Goals:

_____

_____

_____

_____

_____

_____

_____

_____

_____

_____

Team Goals:

_____

_____

_____

_____

_____

_____

_____

_____

_____

_____

Business/Practice Goals:

_____

_____

_____

_____

_____

_____

_____

1-Month I want to accomplish...

_____

_____

_____

_____

_____

_____

3-Months I want to accomplish...

_____

_____

_____

_____

_____

_____

6-Months I want to accomplish...

_____

_____

_____

_____

_____

_____

1 Year I want to accomplish...

_____

_____

_____

_____

_____

_____

_____

_____

5 years I want to accomplish...

_____

_____

_____

_____

_____

_____

_____

_____

Revisit-6 Months

After six months of adopting your new business mindset, you should notice significant improvements: increased revenue, higher treatment plan acceptance, a better office culture, and an increase in your personal income.

If only some, or none, of these have happened, it is time to reflect. Do a self-evaluation. Revisit earlier chapters to gather fresh ideas, reignite your enthusiasm, and get back on track. Perhaps you need a monthly check-in along with a clear plan for the next six months.

Remember, this is your business, your money, and your livelihood. You can choose to keep working without seeing results, or you can commit to being diligent and proactive.

Accountability time: Think of this as a hygiene recall for yourself.

Did you implement everything you said you would?

_____

_____

Have you been staying on track? _____

Overall, how have the new changes worked? What is succeeding, and what still needs adjustment?

_____

_____

_____

_____

_____

_____

What needs to be done to make the next six months more successful and prosperous?

_____

_____

_____

_____

Is your team still aligned with your goals? _____

Are you holding yourself and your team accountable?

_____

_____

_____

_____

_____

Did you complete your 1-month and 3-month goals?

_____

_____

_____

_____

_____

_____

Be sure that along the way, you stay true to your authentic self. Yes, you are a business owner. Yes, you have countless responsibilities on your plate. However, you are also a human being with one life to live. You can be a business owner, a parent, a spouse, a friend, and so much more, all at the same time. One title does not define you.

Live your life in a way that brings you joy and success both inside and outside of "the office." Create a balanced life for yourself and your family. Train your mind to compartmentalize, it will help you maintain a healthy work-life balance.

Are you living a balanced life? _____

Are you joyful or stressed? _____

With that in mind...

Have you kept your personal life and business hours separate?

_____

_____

When off the clock, have you truly stayed off the clock and made time for things that excite and challenge you? _____

Do you have a hobby or activity that makes you happy? If so, what is it? If not, what is something that appeals to you?

_____

_____

Are you spending time with just you? _____

Set a date night with yourself. If business ideas pop into your head, jot them down in your phone's notes app or a journal, then immediately shift your focus back to your personal life.

Set aside a half day with no patients on your schedule to focus on the business side of your practice and complete any patient-related tasks you didn't get to during the week. You could schedule hygiene recalls during this time or have your assistants conduct clear aligner simulator consultations to generate revenue while carving out the time you need to manage the business aspects.

Establishing dedicated hours for business tasks will help you maintain balance and avoid feeling overwhelmed or burnt out. Remember, balance is key to running a successful business while still enjoying your personal life.

To have a more effective six-month review:

Take a quiet moment to reflect on the last six months. Write down your perspective first. Then, speak with your team to gather their thoughts. Group discussions can sometimes lead to groupthink or silence, so consider speaking with team members individually. A quick five-minute conversation in your office between patients can provide valuable insights.

Your perspective on the last six months:

_____

_____

_____

_____

_____

_____

_____

_____

_____

_____

_____

Your team's perspective on the last 6 months.

_____

_____

_____

_____

_____

_____

_____

_____

_____

_____

_____

What has been working? What changes need to be made?

_____

_____

_____

_____

_____

Next 6 Months Goals/To Do List

_____

_____

_____

_____

_____

_____

_____

_____

_____

_____

_____

_____

1 Year Evaluation

When you reach a full year of dedicating yourself to your business, celebrate! Reward yourself with genuine praise, even pat yourself on the heart. Yes, your heart, because it reflects the love and commitment you have shown in investing in yourself.

Embellish the moment. Treat yourself to a nice dinner or buy something special. We often overlook the importance of celebrating our wins and accomplishments, even the small ones along the way. Taking time to acknowledge your progress is so good for your soul.

After a full day of celebrating, it is time to get back to work. Revisit everything from your six-month review and evaluate:

Overall, how have the last six months of the year been?

_____

_____

_____

_____

_____

Same deal...

What is working and not working?

_____

_____

_____

_____

_____

_____

Have you been sticking to your game plan? _____

Are you investing in yourself and your business?

_____

_____

Do Any staff changes need to be made? If so, who?

_____

_____

Are you balancing your home and work life? How so?

_____

_____

_____

Have you been regularly reviewing your revenue, expenses, personal checking, savings account, and investment accounts? Are you putting enough aside to secure success beyond your business?

_____

_____

_____

At the one-year mark, schedule evaluation meetings with your team, accountant, and yourself. Use this time to gather and reflect on feedback to identify areas for growth and improvement.

Notes:

_____

_____

_____

_____

_____

_____

_____

_____

_____

Now, it is time to plan for the upcoming year and reflect on the past one. New Year, New You! How exciting is it that you get to decide how you want this next year to unfold? You have the power to choose what new strategies to implement, the accomplishments you aim to achieve, and the income goals you intend to meet.

What new technology would you like to bring into your practice this year?

_____

_____

_____

Do you have growth goals such as hiring additional staff, adding an operator, or bringing in an associate?

_____

_____

_____

What can you introduce to your practice to generate additional revenue this coming year?

_____

_____

_____

_____

_____

What other ideas can you brainstorm to take your business to the next level?

_____

_____

_____

This Coming Year, I Am Going To...

_____

_____

_____

_____

_____

_____

_____

_____

_____

_____

_____

_____

_____

_____

_____

s

SECTION TWO:

TIPS & TRICKS FOR SUCCESS

SECTION 2

<u>Hygiene</u>

Hygienists are a significant asset to your practice, especially if they can administer injections and work independently without your constant presence. That is why I say, the more, the merrier, though this, of course, depends on how many operatories you have available for hygiene patients.

When it comes to utilizing your team to their fullest potential, this is where hygienists can truly excel. Review your state laws to understand all the ways your hygienists can operate independently and manage their own schedules and patients. During hiring and team meetings, make it clear that this role is essentially their own business within your practice. Offer incentives and compensate them accordingly.

This approach creates a win-win situation: it allows you the freedom to focus on your own schedule while generating additional income for the practice. Meanwhile, hygienists feel empowered and in control of "their business."

❖ **A few ways to set your hygienists up for success:**

- Hire a hygiene assistant to handle periodontal charting, room setup and breakdown, and sterilization.

- Train your hygienists on how to market to their patients using the practice management software, social media, and in-office brochures.

- Provide information upon hiring about proper ergonomics to help protect their long-term health. This not only shows you care but also makes your practice stand out.

- Have the training manager teach hygienists how to use your practice management software (PMS) to schedule patients and pull recall reports for standard six-month recalls and periodontal maintenance patients. Most systems have this functionality.

Hygienist can Treatment Plan their patients, schedule recalls before patients leave the operatory and, should share at least one piece of educational information about your practice with each patient, both verbally and in written form. For example, briefly mention and provide a brochure about services like teeth whitening, Botox/fillers offered in-house, or clear aligners. These products not only improve oral health but also enhance patient care as they age.

Incentive idea: If a hygiene patient commits to an additional service, offer your hygienist 1–3% of the profit as a bonus.

Consideration: Could your hygienists manage a Saturday or evening schedule without your presence?

Hygiene Goals/To do list

State Laws for Hygienist:

_____

_____

_____

_____

_____

_____

_____

_____

_____

How can your hygienists work independently to save you time and boost your revenue?

_____

_____

_____

_____

_____

_____

_____

Goals/To do:

_____

_____

_____

_____

_____

_____

_____

Reviews

Reviews can be a sensitive topic. Some doctors stress over a single "bad" review, while others have found creative ways to handle them, like asking lab technicians to leave 5-star reviews in exchange for more cases or offering free dental work to employees' family members for glowing feedback.

While these strategies might make you chuckle, they highlight an important point: positive reviews are valuable. Word-of-mouth has less influence today, a single negative review can drastically affect how people see your practice. It is a tough reality.

Consider having a team member post something simple and engaging on their social media page, such as:

**"Looking to get my teeth worked on,
any recommendations?"**

You can tweak the wording, but no matter how it is phrased, posts like this always spark reactions. People love sharing their favorite dentists, venting about bad experiences, or even admitting their fear of dental visits, an issue more common than you might think. The talk of Dentist seems to inspire strong feelings: they're either adored, criticized, or feared.

These conversations are eye-opening and show how much reviews matter. That is why being strategic, even a little "creative," with managing reviews is so important. To take control of your reputation,

❖ **Boost positive feedback and minimize the impact of negative reviews:**

- Use patient communication tools to automatically share 4- and 5-star reviews online.
- Send a Google review link directly to patients' phones as they leave the office.
- Offer small rewards, like coffee or donut gift cards, to encourage reviews.
- Automatically feature positive reviews on your website and Healthgrades profile.
- Organize in-office contests, rewarding team members who collect the most 5-star reviews from patients, friends, or family.

- Ask team members to list their most loyal and happy patients, then have your social media lead send a friendly message requesting a review.

Example outreach message:

"[Patient's Name], you always bring such a positive energy to our office, and we love having you here for treatment! Could you do us a favor? The next time you have a great experience with us, would you leave a review on [platform]? It would mean so much if you could mention the doctor or assistant's name, as well as your experience. And of course, a 5-star review helps us out even more!"

You can adjust the wording, but be sure to compliment the patient, ask them to mention specific names, procedures, and their overall experience.

When it comes to negative reviews, they are often based on misunderstandings, like insurance issues, long wait times, or unrealistic expectations. That is why it is crucial to train your team to set clear expectations, communicate effectively, and always work collaboratively with you.

For example, a proactive team member might say:

"[Patient's Name], Dr. [Name] is running a bit behind and will see you in about [minutes]. Would you like a coffee, tea, snack, or warm towel while you wait?"

In this example, effective communication helps manage expectations and ensures patients feel valued.

When calling a patient, always start by asking if it is a good time to talk. For example:

"[Patient's Name], after speaking with your insurance company, they have agreed to cover [specific treatment]. However, they are requesting [$ amount] for your upcoming appointment. Would you still like to proceed with the [procedure name]?"

Be sure to explain the pros, cons, and overall benefits of the procedure. Highlight how much better they will feel once the procedure is completed.

When patients are in the chair, assistants should explain the procedure in a positive but realistic way. Use reassuring language like, "You might feel a little pinch or some pressure," while avoiding trigger words such as pain or injection.

The goal is to set clear expectations, address potential concerns before appointments, and ensure every patient feels heard and cared for.

After the procedure, ask how their experience was with Dr. [Name] and Assistant [Name]. Address any feedback appropriately, then kindly request a review.

Be consistent. Be intentional.

Build a practice centered on patient care.

5-Star How To's

Who is responsible for creating the list of "Great Patients"?

_____

Which platform will you use to feature only 4- and 5-star reviews on your website and social media?

_____

_____

Who is the team member in charge of responding to reviews?

_____

Which platform(s) are your top priority for collecting reviews?

_____

_____

Additional ideas for generating more reviews:

_____

_____

_____

_____

_____

Wealth in Beauty

When thinking of building a million-dollar business, beauty should come to mind. There is incredible potential in the world of beauty. The real question is, are you brave and bold enough to claim your share?

Beauty already is tied into your purpose as a dentist: providing patient-focused care and creating beautiful, healthy smiles. As we both know, when you change a smile, you change a life. A transformed smile does not just improve appearances, it can create an entirely new person.

❖ **Consider this perspective:**

- Have you ever seen patients return for their next visit with their hair and nails done?
- Heard them talk about the confidence they have gained?
- Heard of them finally pursuing a job they once felt unqualified for, all because of their new smile?
- Have you noticed how they're eating healthier now that they can finally chew properly?

A beautiful, healthy smile will spark life-changing transformations.

A healthy smile can do amazing things, and adding a touch of beauty makes it even more exciting. When someone has a beautiful, healthy smile, they often consider other treatments like:

- Teeth whitening
- Orthodontic appliances or clear aligners
- Regular cleanings
- Choosing implants over bridges
- Botox
- Fillers

What if you invited patients to a "**Night of Beauty**"?

Host a monthly event to celebrate beauty. Make it luxurious, classy, and fun. An adult-only gathering that is inclusive of all genders and ages. Invite men, women, young and seasoned to enjoy hors d'oeuvres, bubbly or wine, give-a-ways, and displays of skincare products.

Give-a-ways can be very beneficial to you as well.

❖ **Examples of giveaways:**

- Complimentary teeth whitening at the end of clear aligner treatment
- A Botox and skincare combo package with a free take-home whitening kit
- A free consultation with smile simulation for clear aligners

The goal is to help people feel even more beautiful while earning a nice profit. Bonus: When someone gets Botox or fillers, they often want more! Plus, getting certified to offer these treatments is surprisingly simple.

Search online for "Botox in-person courses for dentists." You can usually find a 1- or 2-day course in your area for under $2,000. These courses often include certifications, marketing tips, training on fillers, and answers to your questions.

❖ **If you are already certified, here are a few tips:**

- Promote your services through emails, your website, and brochures in your office.

- Set up eye-catching displays at the check-in and check-out areas.
- Share before-and-after photos and videos to highlight results.
- Do not offer Botox, fillers, or skincare products for free to your team, friends, or family.

Remember, the goal is to make money, not lose it. The only exception might be your spouse. For your team, consider offering these services at cost with a small markup.

Since the beginning of time, BEAUTY SELLS. When people see other people looking their best, it inspires them to look their best. People naturally want what other happy people have. Display beautiful smiles and transformations throughout your office to drive interest and sales.

"Outer beauty turns the head, but inner beauty turns the heart."

- **Helen J. Russell**

A warm, beautiful smile can do both.

Photos & displays matter.

Wealth in Beauty Goals/To do list

Botox/Filler Certification closest to me:

_____

_____

_____

Marketing plan:

_____

_____

_____

_____

_____

Goals / To do:

_____

_____

_____

_____

_____

_____

_____

Socials

Ah, social media, love it or hate it, it is an essential tool for marketing your business. Remember when we talked about posting for dental recommendations? If you gave it a try, you probably noticed how quickly it became a hot topic.

When it comes to social media, the platform(s) you use do not matter as much as consistent management. Handling it yourself is not recommended, it is time consuming and often gets neglected, which defeats the purpose.

Instead, delegate this responsibility. Have a marketing team member take charge, or hire a freelance social media manager through platforms like Upwork or Fiverr.

Your time is valuable, learn to delegate!

When hiring a social media manager, their creativity, consistency, and knowledge of content are crucial. As with any employee, it is important to oversee their work to ensure they are delivering what you hired them to do.

Each platform has its own style and purpose.

Here is a quick guide:

❖ Facebook

Post three times a week:

- **Personal updates:** Share office happenings, like welcoming a new team member, celebrating a baby, or announcing a promotion. People love hearing good news and staying in the loop, think of this as *"controlled gossip."*

- **Educational content**: Get creative! For example, share a fun "Little Shop of Horrors" reference to explain dental health or highlight how nitrous oxide can make visits less stressful, listing pros and cons. You can also post "Did You Know" facts or unique tips to engage your audience.

- **Subtle marketing**: Promote events like your *"Night of Beauty"* or special offers tied to specific procedures in a low-key, engaging way.

❖ YouTube

People love how-to videos, funny mishaps, and quick entertainment. Search for "Dentist Disasters" and you will find some videos with over 35 million views, it is mind-blowing!

To keep your audience hooked, post YouTube Shorts three times a week. Bonus: As your channel grows, you can even make money from views!

❖ TikTok

Search *"Dentist"* or *"Dental"* and explore different categories to see what content grabs your attention. Pay attention to the number of views to identify what is popular.

❖ Instagram

Similar to TikTok, search for "Dentist" or "Dental" to get ideas and inspiration for posts.

There are many platforms to choose from. Use a search engine to look up "Social Media Platforms." When it comes to deciding which one to use, how to create content, and how often to post, these are important topics to discuss during your interview or consultation with a Social Media Manager. They will work with you to brainstorm ideas. The goal is to educate yourself so you can have an informed conversation during the interview.

Treat this interview process like any other job interview: review resumes, shortlist 3-5 candidates for phone interviews, select 2 people for in-person or video interviews, and then choose the best person for the role.

Once hired, schedule content review meetings at 30 and 60 days. This will be their probationary period. While a 90-day probation is standard, you want to closely monitor the content your social media manager post, as they will be managing your public profiles.

Expect the first few weeks to be spent on research and planning, as your Content/Social Media Manager creates a content posting schedule. They should be compensated for this time. After that, regular posts should start flowing.

By the 30-day mark, you should have around two weeks of content posted. This will give you an idea of what you like, what needs improvement, and what changes to make.

By the 60-day mark, you will know if they are consistently meeting expectations, if they have made the changes you requested, and whether it is time to create another platform profile or consider hiring a different candidate from your shortlist.

Take a few moments to brainstorm, in the next section you will have the opportunity to write down your social media goals. I encourage you to try different platforms, you never know which one will be more successful for you. Do not neglect this part of your business. Online presence can make or break your new patient goals.

"Regrets. You never regret something you tried to do. Pass or fail you know the answer. It is the unknowing in which we regret."

Pro Tip: Cost effective, professional, and incredibly talented creators, designers, and managers for content and pages. Social media Platforms, Google page, Website content, and Marketing:
www.fiverr.com Official Fiverr Website
www.upwork.com Official Upwork Website

Socials Goals/To do list

Platforms of Interest:

_____

_____

_____

_____

Content Creators You Like / Which Platforms Are They On?

_____

_____

_____

_____

Content Manager: In-Office, Virtual, Current Team Member, or Freelance?

_____

_____

Goals/ to do:

_____

_____

_____

_____

Marketing

Marketing is EVERYTHING when it comes to running a successful business. Positive word of mouth does not carry much weight anymore, but negative reviews can feel like heavy brick of fake gold.

Think about the last time you wanted to try a new restaurant. You probably either googled it or got a recommendation from someone who had been there. Did you immediately check the reviews, even if the recommendation came from someone you trust? If someone told you, "I went to this restaurant last night, and it was awful. The service was bad, the food was overpriced, and the quality was terrible." Would you bother to look it up? Honestly, probably not. You would just write it off as a waste of time and money then move on. It is funny how we need validation for positive feedback but then tend to trust the negative right away.

When marketing your business, you want people talking about you. You want them searching for you, reading your reviews, checking out your website, visiting your location, and leaving happy. Ideally, this cycle should keep repeating itself.

I cannot stress this enough: **The experience each patient has from the moment they schedule an appointment to the moment they leave your practice is a marketing tool.** Even if they book their appointment online, the ease of doing so, matters. How they are greeted when they walk into your office, matters. Always remind yourself and your team, the way each team member interacts with a patient can either help or hurt your business.

The way you run your practice will directly affect both your business and personal success.

Now, let's talk about online marketing. Any platform that allows reviews can work in your favor if you use them wisely:

- **Healthgrades** – *Customize your profile.*
- **Zocdoc** – *Extremely popular for patient bookings.*
- **Your website** – *Add reviews and meta tags. Use keywords in your page headings to help search engines find you (e.g., Implants, Botox, sedation). Also, add blogs to boost your SEO.*

- **Social media** – *Likes and followers are like stars: the more you have, the better your reputation looks.*

Patient engagement and communication platforms are worth the investment. They simplify your in-house marketing with automated scheduling (set it and forget it) and templates. Most can target specific patients based on criteria like insurance type, procedure, and age range. This is incredibly valuable because you can create targeted campaigns and set up an entire year's worth of marketing in advance.

__Insurance Types__ – Find the plan that offers the best coverage for procedures like implants. Then, create an educational email about implants that includes something like, "Did you know _____ insurance covers _____ of this procedure?!"

__Holidays__ – Start marketing a month before each holiday. For example, offer teeth whitening specials and share tips to help your patients' smiles shine for family holiday photos.

__Age Ranges__ – Send targeted emails based on age group (these will go to the parent's email on file):

- *Sealants for younger children*
- *Wisdom teeth and braces for teens*
- *Cleanings for college-bound students*
- *Whitening for young adults*
- *Implants and Botox for middle-aged adults*
- *Full Arch reconstruction and removable dentures for middle-aged to elderly patients*

New Patients – *Send a one-page welcome email introducing yourself and your practice before their first appointment, and follow up with a thank-you email afterward.*

The key is to think creatively, use free marketing as much as possible, and take action.

Get Involved Locally – *Go introduce yourself to your neighbors and make connections with local medical professionals, dental specialists, other general dentists, and dental labs in your area. Why? Because it is a great opportunity to build relationships! Business cards and small candy bags can go a long way. For a personal touch, include a one-page introductory letter with the candy bag and your business card.*

Medical Offices – *Provide an introductory letter with helpful information related to their services. For example:*

Pediatricians: Sealants, fillings, crowns

Geriatrics: Chewing and mastication appliances

Cardiologists: Let patients know they need a cleared bill of health before heart or dental surgery.

The goal is low-cost marketing that can lead to valuable connections. You never know when someone will need to utilize services or if what skills, procedures, and qualifications you have to offer such as Botox, your neighbors might not. You want as many people as possible to know who you are and what you have to offer.

Pro Tip: Patient Engagement & Communication Platforms:
www.solutionreach.com Official Solutionreach website
www.demandforce.com Official Demandforce website
www.lh360.com Official Lighthouse 360+ website
www.revenuewell.com Official RevenueWell website
These are a few examples. Google patient engagement and communication platforms for a broader selection.

Marketing Goals/To do list

_____

_____

_____

_____

_____

_____

_____

_____

_____

_____

_____

_____

_____

_____

_____

_____

_____

_____

_____

_____

SECTION THREE:

SUCCESSFULLY BOWING OUT

SECTION 3

Keeping it in the Family

When you find your passion, the thing that excites you, then turn it into a business that makes money, it is a special achievement. You can change lives, give back to your community, and create lasting wealth. Every product or service you have ever bought was made by someone who had an idea and took the risk to start a business. That is exactly what you are doing now: taking risk, making changes to improve yourself, and achieving more.

Ideally, passing your business down to your family is the best outcome. You can build something so remarkable that your children, your nieces and nephews, or even your grandchildren's children will have a head start in life. That is something to be proud of.

However, the person you choose to take over your business must be ready for the hard work of completing dental school, which, as you know, is no easy feat.

When it is time for your successor to step in, make the transition gradual. A successful handover usually takes about 5 years, so it is important to have a clear plan.

❖ **Consider these questions**:

- *Are they business-savvy, or will they need some guidance to take over?*
- *Will you bring in an associate? If so, will it be a family member or someone outside the family?*
- *Do your patients need time to adjust to the new doctor? (The goal is for every patient to stay with the practice.)*
- *What tasks do you need to complete before the transition?*
- *For tax reasons, are you selling the business or gifting it?*
- *What else needs to be done to ensure the business continues to thrive for generations?*

Write down everything that comes to mind and create your transition plan.

Keeping it in the Family Goals/To do list

_____

_____

_____

_____

_____

_____

_____

_____

_____

_____

_____

_____

_____

_____

_____

_____

_____

_____

_____

_____

<u>Selling the Practice – Private Buyer</u>

Build. Build. BUILD! I cannot emphasize this enough. You might have to rely on your retirement savings for 20 years or more, and none of us can predict when we will leave this world.

Earlier in this book, Life After Dental, we talked about how important it is to keep the end goal in mind. The plan now is to create your 5-year strategy so you can make a strong profit when you sell your business.

If you decide to sell your practice to a Dental Support Organization (DSO) or Dental Service Organization (DSO), it is different from selling to a private buyer. We will go into more detail about this in the next chapter, but in short, DSOs care more about location, while private buyers consider several other factors, such as:

- *How established is the business?*
- *What is the potential for generating more income in this location?*
- *What improvements must be made to increase profitability?*

- *What is the current main source of income for the practice?*
- *How many ACTIVE patients are in the database?*

The more you build up your business and have documents proving its value before it goes on the market, the higher the price you can sell for.

In many ways, selling a business is like selling a house, add value, and you can get more value in return. The biggest factor here is time. A realtor can walk through a house and create a "To-Do" list of changes that will increase its value and appeal. These improvements can be made in a few weeks or months. But for a business, it takes time to build that value. That is why the most successful owners give themselves a realistic timeline and a well-thought-out plan.

Starting on a specific date, your goal is to grow your business year after year for the next 5 years. You need to track consistent, profitable growth. Just like a patient will drive an hour to see you, a person will drive an hour or more to a job they love and that pays well. Make your practice so appealing that your buyer falls in love with it and feels they must buy it.

"This is it. This is my new home. This is where I can see myself thriving and being successful."

Let's make you shine, and make a lot of money by creating an exit plan that makes your business highly attractive to buyers.

Pro Tip: Even if you do not plan on selling in the next 5, 10 or 15 years, do not skip over the next section. It is a valuable tool to use for measurable business metrics.

Selling the Practice -Private Buyer

My revamp start date will be: _____

End of Year One...

Profitable growth percentage I aim for is: _____

I will reach this growth goal by tracking each of the following:

- Percentage of New Patients: _____

Top 3 ways to attract New Patients...

_____

_____

_____

- Percentage of Total Hygiene Recalls: _____

Perio recall %: _____ Standard recall % _____

Top 3 ways to increase Hygiene Recalls...

_____

_____

_____

_____

_____

- Percentage of Treatment Plan Acceptance:

Current Treatment Plan Acceptance % _____

Needs to increase by: _____ percent to reach the goal.

According to search engines, the top 3 ways to improve Treatment Plan acceptance are:

_____

_____

_____

_____

Beginning Year Two

The profitable growth percentage should be: _____

What can I implement or build on to increase my value:

_____

_____

_____

_____

_____

_____

_____

_____

- Percentage of New Patients needed: _____
- Percentage of Total Hygiene Recalls needed: _____
- Percentage of Tx Plan Acceptance needed: _____

Brainstorming/Goals for Year Two:

_____

_____

_____

_____

Schedule appointments with yourself, your accountant, your retirement specialist, and anyone else you need to make this transition as successful as possible. Starting in Year One, set your meetings for the beginning and end of each year to stay on track. Create your 5-year plan.

This may seem like a lot of work, but you are already doing most of it. You schedule appointments with your patients in advance, and you have meetings set with your accountant. Now, just schedule those same appointments, but focus them on increasing your value.

You can make a lot of money when you sell your business and while you are building it.

My Retirement Date: _____

Year One: Start: _____   End: _____

Year Two: Start: _____   End: _____

Year Three: Start: _____   End: _____

Year Four: Start: _____   End: _____

Year Five: Start: _____   End: _____

My Practice will be on the Market by: _____

Additional Notes / To do:

_____

_____

_____

_____

_____

_____

_____

_____

_____

Selling the Practice - DSO

Not everyone is meant to be a business owner. Sometimes, life throws unexpected challenges that change the path we are on. Other times, we start out with a lot of drive and energy, only to realize that a better work-life balance, without all the stress, brings more joy than running a company.

Selling your practice to a Dental Support/Service Organization (DSO) can give you more freedom, options and control over the sale. You can sell to a DSO at any point in your career and still negotiate to run the practice as if it were your own, but without the headaches. Some benefits include:

- You can negotiate the terms of your contract. For example, if you agree to a 5-year contract, you can renegotiate when the term ends or choose to leave the company.
- You will get a range of benefits, such as medical, dental, vision, vacation time, retirement plans, sick days, and more.

- DSOs typically offer support, resources, the latest technology, and office remodels.
- You can still create your "Exit Plan" based on your own needs and goals.

The best part: Unlike selling to a private buyer, you do not have to build the value of your business before selling. DSOs have research teams that mainly choose practices based on their location. The sale process is more straightforward and simpler. Whether you decide to sell to a private buyer or a DSO, there is a lot to consider. Making a pros and cons list for both options can help you gain the clarity you need to make the best decision for yourself and your family.

"You get to decide where your time goes, you can either spend it moving forward, or you can spend it putting out fires. Decide. And if you don't decide, others will decide for you."

-Tony Morgan

Selling the Practice – DSO Pros & Cons

<u>Your Personal Retirement Plan</u>

With all the talk about Social Security, whether it will be there, how much you will get, or people thinking their spouse or family will cover retirement, it is time to push those thoughts aside. The truth is, just like with your business, you are the only one who can control your financial future.

Here are a few tough but important questions to ask yourself:

Are you currently investing enough to set yourself up for retirement? _____

Is the amount you're investing enough to live on for 15 or 20 years after you retire? _____

Do you have a financial advisor? _____

Have you read any books on how to use your 401k plan? (Are you educating yourself?) _____

What percentage of each paycheck are you paying yourself first? _____

It does not matter what stage of your career you are in; it is never too late to wake up tomorrow and decide to do better, be better, and have more.

If you are not great at saving money or paying yourself first, start now.

First, **get a payroll company**. If you already have one, great! Pay yourself a percentage of your income.

Second, **set up a High Yield Money Market Account** that is separate from your regular personal bank account. This will be your liquid savings account (money you can access easily). You should have at least three bank accounts: one for your business, one for personal everyday use, and one for your High Yield Money Market savings.

Third, make **saving automatic**. Set up automatic transfers from your everyday personal account to your liquid savings account, also known as a High Yield Money Market account. Choose an amount that you are comfortable with, you can always increase it later.

The last step is to **educate** yourself. READ! Let's say you're ready to hire a financial advisor (which you should do right away). How will you know if they are working for you or just making a profit off your money if you cannot have an informed conversation with them?

After six months, build on your financial portfolio. Increase your savings percentage, open an investment account, or buy Treasury or I-Bonds.

Before making any new investments, consult your financial advisor and make sure you fully understand what you are getting into. Without the right knowledge, you could end up losing money.

Here are the books I recommend reading, in this order, to help educate yourself on...

Paying myself first/ Setting a percentage aside.

"The Richest Man in Babylon"
Original Edition by George S. Clason

Making savings automatic.

"The Automatic Millionaire"
by David Bach

Finding Financial Advisors/Learning about investing.

"Money Master The Game"
by Tony Robbins

"The Intelligent Investor" Revised Edition
By Benjamin Graham

Although lengthy, I strongly recommend reading each book in full taking one chapter at a time highlighting or underlining what brings value to you. Then, six months to a year down the road, rereading only the highlighted areas as a refresher.

Here's an example of how your investments should start, if pay is $1000 a week:
- 10% for investing
- 10% for liquid savings
- 70% for bills
- the last 10% is for fun

Creating memories is just as important as saving and investing money. Take the trip. Buy the outfit. Donate to something you care about. Do things that bring joy to

your life. If all you do is work just to save, you will get burnt out and frustrated.

It is the same as working just to keep working, what is the point? It is crucial to take the time now to ensure you are setting yourself up for retirement with financial freedom.

Pro Tip*: from **Millionaire Business Owners:***
Your kids, starting as a teenager, and immediate family should always be on your payroll and 401k.

Your Personal Retirement Plan Goals/To do list

Payroll company: _____

Amount % I will save each paycheck: _____

My Financial Advisor is: _____

I will pay off my car by: _____

I will pay off my house by _____

Book I will read on 401k plans:

_____

Books on running successful Small Businesses:

_____

_____

_____

_____

_____

Book on Small Business Taxes:

_____

_____

_____

Retirement Goals:

_____

_____

_____

_____

_____

_____

_____

_____

_____

_____

_____

_____

_____

_____

_____

_____

_____

_____

_____

_____

SECTION FOUR:

EXTRA MILE = EXTRA WEALTH

SECTION 4

Making Yourself Known

When marketing your business, your goal is to make as many people in your community, or within a certain distance from your business, aware of the services you offer and make those services appealing enough to attract valuable customers. In most dental marketing, there might be a short description of who you are, but the focus is usually on the services or specials offered. This is why "Making Yourself Known" is so important.

This is about you, and only you. Along with promoting your business, your goal should be to help as many people as possible understand who you are and why you do what you do. The "Why" is what will make you stand out from your colleagues. Have a story. Share your story. Introduce yourself and your story as often as possible.

To explain the idea of taking a "Day for Business," use the morning for business tasks and the afternoon for introducing yourself. Taking one or two days each month, every month, will pay off greatly in the long run.

You might think this sounds repetitive or wonder, "Who am I going to introduce myself to every month?" or "What impact could this possibly have on my business?"

Great questions! You can Introduce yourself to...

- *Other General Dental Practitioners: Get to know your colleagues. You never know who you might be able to help or who could help you.*
- *Dental Specialists (Endodontists, Oral & Maxillofacial Surgeons, Pediatric Dentists): Make connections with specialists within a one-hour radius. Patients are willing to travel and may be looking for new referral relationships. Tip: Be sure to bring a gift basket when meeting them.*
- *Dental Board Members: They often have valuable knowledge and connections.*
- *Local Dental Associations: This includes both State and County associations. Find out when their meetings are held, and attend*

them. If you are feeling bold, consider finding a topic to speak about.

- *Anyone Hosting Continuing Education (CE) Events: Attend these events. Oral Surgeons and dental labs often host CE events, and even some larger general practices do. You'd be surprised at how many other general practitioners attend.*

- *Dental Lab Owners and Their Staff: Get to know the lab owners and those they employ: Operation Managers, Technicians, Drivers, etc.*

- *Local Dental Conferences: Make it a point to meet and connect with 1 to 3 colleagues at each conference. Ask them engaging questions to gain business-building insights. For example:*
    - *What do you think was a mistake you made when you first started out?*
    - *If you could name one factor that had the biggest impact on your practice's success, what would it be?*

The key point here is to set aside time and make an effort to get to know your dental community, and allow them to get to know you. You never know which relationship or opportunity could take you to the next level. Put yourself out there. Share your story. Be creative. Listen to others' stories. Learn from their wisdom to help you grow. Be genuine, and truly connect with your colleagues and peers in the dental field.

"When dealing with people, remember you are not dealing with creatures of logic, but creatures of emotion."

-Dale Carnegie

Pro Tip: If you have the meeting space, consider hosting an event at your practice. It will be a nice, discrete way to show off, aka market, your business accomplishments and make yourself more welcoming to your colleagues.

Extra Mile=Extra Wealth:
Make Yourself Known: Goals/To do list

3 Specialists in my area:

_____

_____

_____

State Dental Board Meeting Date: _____

My and surrounding County Dental Association Meetings:

_____

_____

_____

_____

3 Dental Labs near me:

_____

_____

_____

3 local Continuing Education Host:

_____

_____

_____

Other Goals:

_____

_____

_____

_____

_____

_____

_____

_____

Additional Notes:

_____

_____

_____

_____

_____

_____

_____

Investing In You

Where are you at right now in your career?

- Are you running your own practice?
- Still in dental school?
- An associate in a practice?
- Nearing retirement?
- Getting ready to apply to dental schools?

Being an associate means you are helping someone else build their wealth. Going through dental school and not starting your own practice will only make someone else rich. Having a successful practice and then working until you retire does not benefit you or your family.

No matter where you are, you have already made an investment in yourself to get here. You know how to invest in yourself. The question is:

What is the purpose behind all your hard work and dedication to get where you are now?

Now is the time to reinvest in yourself. Create small wins every day. Follow through on what you say you'll do. Are you going to eat healthier? Then eat healthy. Are you going to start going to the gym? Then go. Are you going to get rid of that staff member who has been bothering you? Let them go.

Set small goals. Check them off as you accomplish them. Let go of control and learn to delegate. Improve both your personal life and your business. Sign up for a continuing education course. Buy flowers for the check-in/check-out area. Apply to top schools. Add an educational or motivational figure you admire to your social media. Remove someone from your life who negatively affects you.

Do something today that makes you happy. What small change can you make to be healthier? How can you earn some extra money? Look around your bedroom or office, what has been bothering you? Fix it. Change it. What can you do today to make a positive difference?

"The best investment you can make is in yourself. It pays the best interest."

-Unknown

Extra Mile=Extra Wealth:
Invest in Yourself: Goals/To-Do List

I will invest in myself by...

_____

_____

_____

_____

_____

_____

_____

_____

_____

_____

_____

_____

_____

_____

_____

_____

_____

_____

_____

<u>Patient-Centric Practice</u>

You have probably heard the saying, "There are three sides to every story: your side, their side, and the truth." It seems like everyone has their own view of what it means to have a patient-centered practice.

Before we dive in, take a moment to write down what a patient-centered practice means to you. Be specific.

_____

_____

_____

_____

_____

_____

_____

_____

_____

_____

_____

_____

_____

_____

Read the dialogue below. The conversation started with me asking a friend when she last went to the dentist, then asking why it had been so long.

Real story:

Her response: "It's painful, my teeth are sensitive."

Me: "What part of getting your teeth cleaned bothers you the most?"

Her: "The water and the scraping. And it's the way they treat you. It's like they don't believe you. No one seems to care."

Making the first appointment:

Receptionist: "Ms. (insert name), we have you scheduled for (day/time). Are there any concerns or fears you have about getting your teeth cleaned?"

Her: "Yes, the water squirter and the scraping."

Receptionist: "Thank you for letting me know. I'll make a note of that for your appointment."

Me asking my friend: "If the person making your appointment addressed your concerns like this, would that make you feel a bit more at ease?"

She replied: "YES, it would."

Upon Arrival...

Receptionist: "Hi, Ms. (insert name). Thank you for coming in today. I saw your notes about sensitivity to scraping and water. We've shared this with your hygienist, and we have a new technique that we think will make you more comfortable."

Receptionist: (5 minutes later) "Your hygienist is on time and will be out at (your appointment time) to take you back. Would you like something to drink, a warm towel, or use the restroom before we begin?"

Me asking my friend:

"If the front desk addressed your concerns like this, kept you informed about your wait time, and offered you something, would it help you feel more at ease?"

She replied: "Yeah, it would."

Walking to the Back with the Hygienist...

Hygienist: "Hi, Ms. (insert name), my name is (insert name). I've read your notes, and I want to make sure, we address all of your concerns. Can I ask you a few questions?"

Hygienist: "After you brush your teeth at home, does swishing with water bother you?"

Her: "No, I use warm water and gently swish."

Hygienist: "Great. What if we do not use the water squirter and instead just do a gentle warm water rinse after the cleaning to remove the gritty feeling? I can have a small cup ready with water at your preferred temperature. Would that work better for you?"

Her: "Yes, thank you, that would make me feel better."

Hygienist: "Great. Now that we have a possible solution for your water sensitivity, may I ask about your sensitivity to scraping?"

Hygienist: "Are both the top and bottom teeth sensitive, or is it just certain areas? What specifically bothers you about the scraping?"

Her: "No, nothing on my lower teeth bothers me. It's just the two sides next to my front teeth," (she points to them). "And it's the metal scraper."

Hygienist: "Okay, perfect. I have a new plastic tool I can use for those sensitive areas. I will use it on those spots and the standard instruments, very gently, for the rest of your teeth. I will check in with you every step of the way. Would it be okay if we try this new technique to see if it makes you more comfortable?"

Her: "Yes, that sounds much better. Thank you!"

Me asking my friend:

"If your hygienist addressed both your water and scraping concerns by explaining new techniques, asking exactly what bothers you, and then discussing a solution, would that help you feel even more at ease?"

She replied: "YES, it would!"

As you can see in this conversation, by simply asking a few questions, changing the way you word things, explaining each step, and showing the patient that their time and concerns matter, you greatly increase the chances that the patient will have a positive experience. This could lead to a better review and, most importantly, them booking their next appointment.

Going the extra mile does not always require a huge investment of time or money. Sure, you can install TVs, offer headphones, place flowers around your office, or even use scents in the ventilation system. But you can also train your staff to spend a little more time with each patient and take the extra step to really listen and address their needs.

A few very simple tips...

- Scheduling by Phone: Address the patient by name and ask if they have any concerns.
- Scheduling Online: Call the patient to confirm and address any concerns. Make sure patients hear a voice before their appointment – it will make it feel more personal and memorable.
- Upon Arrival: Greet the patient by name. If you did not reach them before, acknowledge their concerns or ask them in person.
- While the Patient is Waiting: Give updates, offer a snack, a warm towel, a

drink (warm or cool), or access to the restroom. Address the patient by name.

- When the Assistant or Hygienist Walks the Patient Back: Address any concerns, ask what their plans are after the appointment, and engage in conversation. Be the comforting person who makes them feel at ease.

- You, Their Doctor: Be warm, address their concerns, and gently explain the procedure and how it will benefit them.

- After Numbing: Have your assistant stay in the room. Make a note in the chart about any important small talk (e.g., just married, upcoming surgery, vacation). Use one piece of conversation to follow up on their next visit.

Each patient should feel like they are your only patient. Keeping in mind, patients are people.

People-Centered Practice

Extra Mile=Extra Wealth:
Creating a Patient-Centered Practice

I can make my practice more patient-centered by

_____

_____

_____

_____

_____

When scheduling appointments, my team will...

_____

_____

_____

_____

When patient is in the reception/waiting area, my team will...

_____

_____

_____

_____

_____

_____

When patient is in the treatment room, my team will...

_____

_____

Is there anything else you can think of to help make your patients feel more comfortable, special, and leave your office feeling good about their visit?

_____

_____

_____

_____

_____

_____

_____

Even if you are an associate, you still have your own assistant, your own patients, and the chance to do your own follow-ups. What changes can you make?

_____

_____

_____

_____

Additional Thoughts:

_____

_____

_____

_____

_____

_____

_____

_____

"Spread love everywhere you go. Let no one ever come to you without leaving happier"

-Mother Teresa

Final Thoughts

This is your livelihood. You have the power to shape it however you want. No matter where you are in your career or life, you can decide today is the day to make a change. So, go for it!

A few tips to leave you with:

- Do not procrastinate. Follow through on every decision you make.
- Set goals.
- Make appointments with yourself.
- Add reminders to your phone and calendar.
- Read books to improve your health and wealth.
- Keep working on becoming the best version of yourself.
- Listen to motivational speakers EVERYDAY.
- When you are at work, be fully present.

When you are not at work, enjoy your life. Be a person, not just a dentist. If work-related thoughts pop up, quickly jot them down in your phone or on paper, then move on. And, most importantly...Be PROUD of you! I am.

Daily reminder:

What is the point of owning a business if you are not also investing in yourself?

ACKNOWLEDGEMENTS

In my 20+ years in the dental field, from Dental Assisting School to where I am today, I'm incredibly grateful for the relationships I've built, the friendships I've made, the guidance I've received, and the lessons I've learned.

A few shoutouts...

- **Mary and Maria** – I will always cherish the bonds we formed, the friendly competition that pushed us, and the good times we had in Dental Assisting School. This was the start of a life we never knew we needed. Cheers to us!

- **Lori Bernardo** – My Dental Momma and Mentor, you shaped me into the dental professional, person, and salesperson I was meant to be. I'll never forget when you told me to check my pay stub for the first time, that rainy day you came into town, and when I placed the lei over your head, making my promise to you. These will always be treasured memories. Thank you for believing in me and encouraging me every step of the way in my first "Big Girl" job, which led to opportunities I never imagined. I truly appreciate you!

- **Mark Choi – Owner and CEO of Infinia Dental Lab, Germantown, MD** – Working with you for over three years was challenging in the best ways. I gained a fascinating behind-the-scenes view of what I call "The

CHANGE A SMILE, CHANGE A LIFE   STEPHANIE WELKER

Full Arch Reconstruction Mastermind." Your passion, skills, knowledge, technological expertise, and genuine care for the patient/surgeon/restorative doctor relationship are unmatched. Watching your business grow from nine employees to over 40, and seeing your vision come to life, has been truly inspiring. I've learned so much from you. Thank you!

- **Dr. Michael Schwartz, Dr. Julius Hyatt, and Jackie-Maryland Center for Oral Surgery and Dental Implants, Owings Mills, MD** – This is the first office where I truly wanted to be 100% on top of my skills and knowledge, aligning with the best in the industry. The discipline, accountability, and structure I learned here showed me how a dental practice and its people need to operate for continued growth and success. These surgeons are truly amazing, with great business minds and an incredible ability to help others learn and grow. They're by far the best I've had the pleasure of working with. Side note: The holiday parties and Continuing Education events they host are unmatched! Thank you all!!

- **Jinxy and Amy** – Your friendship, support, fun times, adventures, and constant encouragement to be myself are what keep me grounded and positive. I will always cherish you both. Much love!

- **Melissa** – Thank you for being my friend for over 40 years, and for asking me what I was writing a book about while we were eating chips and salsa. That conversation led to "The Patient Experience," which will be my second book. Love you, girl!

- **Amiee Calderon (Fiverr)** {aimeecalderon055@gmail.com}- Thank you so very much for your talent and expertise in editing and formatting. The professionalism and bringing this book to life is credited to you. I look forward to working with you in the near future.

- **Yasir Nadeem – (Fiverr) Cover Art & Design** Impeccable work. Very timely. Such a pleasure.

Felicity and Serenity – My beautiful girls! You both are the reason behind my drive to build generational wealth with integrity and a pure heart. My goal is to show you both that no matter where you come from, what your childhood was like, or how others treat you, your worth is determined by your own choices and experiences. It is up to you to decide who you will become and the path you will take. I will always support you and do everything I can to help you be more, do more, and have more. You may think that John or your dad was the love of my life, but they were not. It will always be the both of you, for exactly who you are. I love you, my Sweet Serenity! I love you, my Feisty Felicity!

Thank you to everyone who helped bring this book to life!

Disclaimer:

I do not have any affiliations with the books or websites mentioned.

Next up from the Author...

A step-by-step interactive guide on personal growth, success, and building your investment profile for the lay person.

"One Step, The First Step"

"Everything in Life Can Be Accomplished in Step One"

For booking speaking events, consultations, and sharing success stories:

AuthorStephanieWelker@Gmail.com

A portion of the proceeds goes towards teeth care packages for lower income communities and women's shelters.

Thank you for your purchase!

www.ingramcontent.com/pod-product-compliance
Lightning Source LLC
Chambersburg PA
CBHW051532120626
46551CB00012B/1184